FEB   2016

Performing Live

Matt Anniss

A+
Smart Apple Media

Published by Smart Apple Media, an imprint of
Black Rabbit Books
P.O. Box 3263, Mankato, Minnesota 56002
www.smartapplemedia.com

Published by arrangement with the Watts Publishing Group LTD, London.

Library of Congress Cataloging-in-Publication Data
Anniss, Matt.
  Performing live / by Matt Anniss.
    pages cm. – (The music scene)
  Summary: "Explains the business behind live musical performances, from small coffee shop gigs to over-the-top arena spectaculars. Explains what it's like to be on tour, how managers book gigs, and how roadies help set up shows. Case studies highlight the Rolling Stones long touring career, Michael Eavis's charity festivals, media giant Live Nation, and the mega-tour of U2"– Provided by publisher.
  Includes index.
  ISBN 978-1-59920-913-5 (library binding)
  1. Rock music–Vocational guidance–Juvenile literature. 2. Rock groups–Performances–Juvenile literature. 3. Music–Performance–Juvenile literature. I. Title.
  ML3795.A855 2015
  781.4'3–dc23

                    2013022574

ISBN 978-1-59920-913-5 (library binding)
ISBN 978-1-62588-593-7 (eBook)

Dewey Classification: 781.4'3

Printed in the United States by CG Book Printers
North Mankato, Minnesota

PO 1720
PO 2-2015

9 8 7 6 5 4 3 2 1

Acknowledgments:
The publisher would like to thank the following for permission to reproduce photographs: Dreamstime: Ahmet Ihsan Ariturk 26–27, Dario Diament 43t, Dragos Daniel Iliescu 27cr, Imagecollect 31bl, Pavel Losevsky 9br, Michael Lunceford 19br, Nordjordet 28bl, Prestong 40tr, Valentino Visentini 32bl; Istock: Anthony Brown 24cr, Steve Debenport 31tr; Lollapalozza.com: Cambria Harkey 23b; Rex Features: 38tr, James Fortune 12bl, Adrian Sherratt 25tr, Richard Young 39br; Shutterstock: Arvzdix 35tr, 41bl, Auremar 30tr, Carl Bjorklund 17tl, Maxim Blinkov 17cr, ChinellatoPhoto 41tr, Dfree 16bc, Andreas Gradin 6tr, Alan Heartfield 22tr, Gynnis Jones 18tr, Konstantynov cover, Aija Lehtonen 34bl, R. Gino Santa Maria 15b, Olly 14tr, Losevsky Pavel 42bl, Kristina Postnikova 10bl, Lev Radin 9tl, 21tr, Nikola Spasenoski 7b, 22bl, Ronald Sumners 10tr, TDC Photography 29br, Valeria73 5br, 36–37; Wikipedia: John Stephen Dwyer 33tl, Magnushk 14bl, Rich Niewiroski Jr 36bl, Hilary Perkins 8bl, Kenny Sun 20b, Tabercil 11cr.

Every attempt has been made to clear copyright. Should there be any inadvertent omission please apply to the publisher for rectification.

CONTENTS

CHAPTER ONE

GOING LIVE!

In a vast arena, a crowd of thousands waits. Clutching glossy **tour** programs, they scope out the arrival of their musical heroes. A sudden flash of light greets tonight's audience, and so begins one of the best live acts in the world. With a drum roll, the count in, and the first electric chord sounding, a deafening roar rolls through the arena.

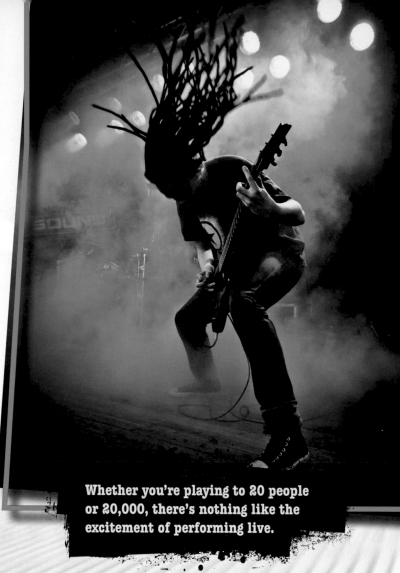

Whether you're playing to 20 people or 20,000, there's nothing like the excitement of performing live.

Just Another Gig

For some in the crowd, this will be a once in a lifetime event—a rare chance to see their favorite band perform. For the band involved, it is likely to be one date on a long tour that could take them to all corners of the world.

Right Here, Right Now

Live music events happen every day around the world. A **gig** can vary in size and splendor. It might be a legendary rock band playing in a sports stadium, but it's just as likely to be a group of local **amateurs** playing to a handful of people in a coffee shop.

Feel-good Feeling

Anyone who has ever performed live music will tell you what a great rush it is. Experiencing the crowd respond to a song or solo performance is hugely exhilarating. Being part of a musical group, be it a rock band, **hip-hop** crew, or classical orchestra, gives a feel-good vibe. If you hit the right notes, everyone feels great.

The Scoop

Concerts and live performances are a big money-maker for the music industry. In recent years, the live music scene has grown rapidly. In 2013, it was estimated that worldwide ticket sales topped a staggering $15 billion.

Love of Live

For many people, it is this good feeling that makes performing live so appealing. While the best live performers can earn millions of dollars, most musicians will barely earn enough to live. Many others won't earn a penny from their performances, but continue to play gigs in their spare time just for the fun of it.

Huge Industry

It is not just performers who can make a living off of live music. The concert industry provides work for millions of people worldwide.

Band managers, concert promoters, sound technicians, instrument makers, costume designers, lighting specialists, security staff, and bus drivers are all part of the live music industry.

When people see their favorite bands play live, there's a huge amount of anticipation— something musicians can feed off to help them put on a great performance.

GOING SOLO

Anyone with a degree of musical talent can perform live. You don't need to be the best musician in the world; you just need to know enough **chords**, **riffs**, or solos to get by, along with a little stage presence. Some of the world's best-known musicians started out this way, playing low-key gigs.

Busker Beginnings

One popular way for solo performers to get experience is to go out **busking**. This is when people play on street corners or in subway stations, performing short sets of songs or **instrumentals** to passing members of the public. Buskers can be found showcasing their talents in many towns and cities. If people like what they hear, they sometimes donate loose change to the musician as a way of showing their appreciation.

The Road to Stardom

Many famous singers and musicians have started their musical careers as weekend buskers. British singer-songwriter James Morrison first performed as a teenage busker in Cornwall, while Canadian rock band Barenaked Ladies busked for years before being offered their first **recording contract**.

Like many musicians, James Morrison had to work hard for stardom, working his way up from singing on the streets to headlining massive music festivals.

Open Mic

Another good way for solo performers to begin is to get a spot at an "open-mic night." These are concerts held at small **venues** designed to showcase new and inexperienced musicians. Anyone can sign up and do a 10- or 15-minute live performance, regardless of whether they've played live before.

Step It Up

After gaining experience on the open-mic circuit, good solo performers may start to pick up bookings to play at other venues in their town or local music festivals. As they gain publicity, they may even get asked to play at more widespread locations.

On the Up

Many small venues have a designated open-mic night every week. There's no limit to how many times you can perform, so many musicians return to the same venue on a regular basis. If they impress the audience, the venue manager might book them to play their own small concert.

The Scoop

US singer-songwriter Gavin DeGraw spent years perfecting his performance skills at open-mic nights and **acoustic** music clubs in New York City. In 2002, he was discovered by music industry executive Clive Davis and offered a recording contract. A year later, his debut album, Chariot, topped the charts.

Performing at small open-mic nights is one way to gain stage experience in front of an audience.

BAND PERFORMERS

Not everyone wants to perform alone. For many people, being in a band offers a more attractive route into live performance. You still get to play music live, but you're with a group of friends. You share the highs and lows, making it a less lonely experience.

Good chemistry between members is vital to the success of any band.

Band Basics

Because a band is a group of musicians, there's room for people who play different instruments. But for a band to be successful, everyone has to play an equal part. The ability to make different voices and instruments sound great together is what separates the bands who "make it" from those who never will.

Fighting it Out

Ambitious bands that write their own music have to follow a similar path as solo performers. Many get their first break at "battle of the bands" competitions, which are the band equivalent of open-mic nights. If they impress the crowd and the judges, they will usually be offered other performance slots at the same venue.

Many bands have enjoyed international success after being discovered at local "battle of the bands" competitions.

Get in the Van

After dominating their local scene, many bands will pick up bookings outside their town. They might even get enough bookings to go on tour—a series of concerts around the country.

To save money, many bands will drive from gig to gig in a van, taking their equipment with them. Some will even sleep in the van!

Stagecraft

Many musicians compare the time logged on their local music scene to serving an **apprenticeship**. It can take years of playing small, local venues for a band to build up a loyal following. Playing this many gigs allows bands to improve their performance skills before playing bigger and better venues later in their careers. With time, not only will their musical skills be razor-sharp, their stage presence and audience interactions will have improved as well.

The Scoop

In 2011, a Canadian boogie rock band called The Sheepdogs won an international battle of the bands competition with a twist. Readers of the famous US music magazine Rolling Stone were asked to give an unknown band a break in a contest to choose the cover. The Sheepdogs' prize included a contract with Atlantic Records, as well as being the first unsigned band ever to grace the magazine's front cover.

The Rolling Stones

Very few bands have played as many concerts as rock icons The Rolling Stones. Since first performing live in London in 1962, the group has been on more than 40 concert tours. Today, they continue to perform live, 50 years after first taking the stage.

The Rolling Stones have sold an estimated 200 million albums, and three of their tours made the top 10 highest grossing tours of all time.

Club Beginnings

The Rolling Stones had to work hard to achieve fame and worldwide success. Early in their career, they were given a weekly **residency** at a London venue called The Crawdaddy Club, where they developed their skills and built up a strong **fan base**.

Tour Tales

The Rolling Stones went on their first tour of the UK in the autumn of 1963. In the following two years, they toured the UK five more times, playing nearly 150 concerts. This relentless schedule helped them to become one of the most entertaining bands on the planet.

Live and Loving It

By the 1970s, The Rolling Stones had sold enough records and played enough concerts to retire as multimillionaires. However, their love for the music and the thrill of performing keeps them coming back for more.

Record Tours

Their *A Bigger Bang*, tour took place over three years between 2005 and 2007. In that time, they played 147 concerts

Deadly Gig

In 1969, a Rolling Stones gig at the Altamont Raceway in northern California had to be stopped because of rioting and fights between concertgoers and members of a local Hells Angels motorcycle group. One person died and many others were injured. Footage of the concert was included in a film about the band called *Gimme Shelter*.

around the world, sometimes to crowds of up to 50,000 people. Ticket sales from the tour earned the band nearly $600 million.

For the Love of Music

Every member of The Rolling Stones is a multimillionaire, and so the concept of singing for their supper is no longer a part of the equation. They tour because they enjoy performing live to large crowds. Now in their seventies, their appetite for playing their songs is as strong as ever.

TIMELINE: The Rolling Stones

1962: Perform their first ever concert at The Marquee Club, London
1964: Tour the US for the first time
1969: Fan killed amid violence at free concert at Altamont Raceway in California
1972: A Rolling Stones concert at the Los Angeles Forum raises more than $200,000 for charity

1989: Conclude their *Steel Wheels* tour with 10 dates at the Tokyo Dome
2006: Become the first British band to play the Super Bowl half-time show
2007: Play the Isle of Wight Festival, their first performance at a music festival in more than 30 years
2011: Release a DVD of unseen footage from their 1968 US tour

13

THE PROFESSIONALS

There's more to live music than famous bands, pop stars, and solo performers. There's another group of musicians who often go unmentioned, but without whose contribution the scene would not exist. These are the professionals.

Session Musicians

Professional musicians exist in many different areas of the music scene. Some, known as **session musicians**, can be hired by performers to complete their **backing band** for concert tours and festival appearances. Session musicians are extremely talented. Because they are not attached to one band or artist, they are skilled in many different musical styles.

Top session drummers are in high demand, and can make a very good living by playing for a number of different bands.

Solid Career

Session musicians are fundamental elements to the music industry, and so this can be a solid career path. Because their fortunes aren't tied to the success of one CD or concert tour, the world's best session musicians can enjoy long and successful careers. Session musician Leland Sklar has recorded tracks with artists ranging from Donna Summer to James Taylor to Robbie Williams.

Bassist Leland Sklar has played as a session musician on thousands of records over the course of his 45-year career.

The Long Game

Over the course of the last 50 years, many session musicians and bands have shaped the history of popular music. A band called MFSB was **integral** to the development of the disco sound, providing backing for singers and vocal groups of the 1970s and '80s, while Los Angeles-based outfit The Wrecking Crew were so **influential**, they were given a place in the Music Hall of Fame in 2007.

Variety of Jobs

There are a number of other performing opportunities for professional musicians. Some television shows will employ a **house band** to perform music, while some plays, such as **musicals**, require a number of musicians. If you're a talented musician and want to perform live, these are options to pursue.

The Scoop

Some session musicians find fame in their own right. After playing on stage with Amy Winehouse, The Haggis Horns were asked by Mark Ronson to play on his *Version* album. The CD was a worldwide success and since then, the band has toured the world headlining concerts in the US and Europe.

Session musicians don't just play on records and CDs—often, they get to go out on tour as part of a solo artist's backing band.

BEAT MASTERS

Music made using traditional and electric instruments has been performed for many years. However, it's only in recent times that the technology has existed for electronically produced music to be performed live.

Studio Music

When electronic dance music first became popular in the 1980s, it was very difficult to perform. When they wrote songs, **electronic musicians** did not expect to have to perform them. Instead, they recorded futuristic tracks that could be released on records or CDs. These were then played in clubs by DJs.

With their flashing "robot head" masks and pounding dance floor beats, Daft Punk revolutionized the way dance music was performed live.

Computer Music

In the early days of hip-hop, house, and techno, tracks were made using equipment that hadn't really been designed for live performance, such as drum machines, **digital samplers**, and computers. Many people who made dance music and hip-hop weren't trained musicians. Instead, they created their songs by a process of trial and error.

Live Music

In the 1990s, dance music became more popular. Fans of dance acts such as The Chemical Brothers, The Crystal Method, Underworld, and Daft Punk expected to be able to see them perform their songs live. These bands and others rose to the challenge, using powerful new computers, **synthesizers**, and drum machines to re-create their music at festivals and other big events.

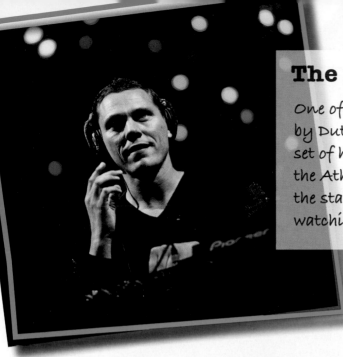

The Scoop

One of the biggest ever dance gigs was performed by Dutch DJ Tiësto in 2004. He played a short set of his own tracks at the opening ceremony of the Athens Olympics. There were 80,000 people in the stadium, and hundreds of millions of people watching around the world via television.

DJs as Musicians

Today, technology allows DJs to turn their sets into a "proper" live performance. Using a laptop computer and software programs such as Ableton Live or Serato Scratch Live, DJs can control every element of the tracks they play. They can change the beats, alter synthesizer loops, and even replace sounds, all in real time.

In recent years, new computer software programs have blurred the boundaries between DJing and live performance.

Performance Pioneer

One of the first DJs to see the potential of DJ performance software was Ralph Lawson, the creator of 2020 Vision Recordings. He put together a band called 2020 Soundsystem in 2004. It featured three musicians performing live drums, keyboard, and bass.

Lawson controlled what the audience heard using his laptop and a DJ mixer. Each show was performed as a nonstop DJ set with a blend of live songs, recorded dance tracks, and electronic loops. Their first album, No Order, included a live CD from Spain's Sonar Festival in 2006.

CHAPTER TWO

LIVE ON STAGE

While enormous stadium-sized concerts from world-famous rock and pop stars make the headlines, most live music is performed in small venues. Every city in the world has its own live music scene. These local settings are at the heart of the live music industry.

What's On?

Take a look at the entertainment events listed in your local newspaper, and you should find a lineup of gigs and concerts going on in your town. The musicians performing at these venues range from inexperienced singers to seasoned artists.

Lots of Venues

In the UK, there are nearly 85,000 places where people can attend live shows on a regular basis. In the US, the number is in the hundreds of thousands. Although some of these are well-established concert halls, theaters, or arenas, most are more scaled down.

Thriving local music scenes are the lifeblood of the live performance scene—without them, many musicians would never get their "big break."

The Scoop

The town of Austin, Texas, holds a unique record. It has more live music venues per person than any other place in the US. It has more than 200 venues to serve 790,000 people—that's one venue for every 4,000 people who live in the city!

Local Heroes

The local live music scenes that exist throughout the world operate in isolation. That means they would exist even if famous bands didn't pass through the city on one of their tours. These scenes are run by local musicians, **promoters**, and venue owners purely to entertain their community.

On the Up

More people are spending money to watch singers and bands perform live than ever before. Live music is among the most popular leisure activities of our times, and it's getting more popular. In 2010, money earned from concert tickets overtook money earned from CD and download sales for the very first time. Music festivals, such as SXSW in Austin, Texas, are becoming more poular, too, as are local music scenes. Since live sets are where all performers take their first steps into the limelight, it's great news for anyone who dreams of playing music for a living.

Local Action

For a band or singer to become successful, they must first conquer their local live music scene. Arctic Monkeys may have become famous over the Internet after posting songs on Myspace, but they already had a big fan base in their home city of Sheffield in the UK.

The band first became popular in small clubs that attracted young music fans eager to hear new and unknown bands.

Performances from artists such as Macy Gray at the SXSW festival have helped Austin, Texas, become America's undisputed live music capital.

ON TOUR

When an artist or band has gained a reputation in their local music scene, there are two routes forward: record their music, or go on a regional or national concert tour. This is a series of performances in a number of different cities over an established period of time.

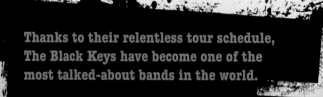

Thanks to their relentless tour schedule, The Black Keys have become one of the most talked-about bands in the world.

Good to Go

Most musicians with dreams of success hire a manager, someone who can help them make it big. A manager arranges for them to record their first songs. For those songs to sell well, the artist must promote them. Traditionally, this has meant going on a concert tour. Bands such as The Black Keys focus on tours to keep their fans' interest.

The First Tour

Ambitious performers dream of going on their first tour. If venues around the country are willing to book you, it means they think they will be able to sell enough tickets to make a profit.

Tour Time

Tours can vary in length enormously, depending on how well a performer is known and how much demand there is to see them play. Established bands with a successful track record may travel throughout the country for a few months, while new bands with just one CD to their name may only do a handful of concerts over a couple of weeks.

Tiring Days

The life of a touring band can be relentless. After playing a concert, they often get back to their hotel well after midnight. Early the next morning, they will have to travel to their next destination, which could be hundreds or thousands of miles away.

In Demand

When they arrive at their next stop, bands have little time to rest. They set up their equipment, **soundcheck** (run through a few songs to make sure their instruments sound right), eat, and get dressed. They may also have to fit in interviews with local journalists and meet **VIP guests**—all within a few short hours. Once they've finished performing, the cycle begins again.

Small Time

Often, a band's first concert tour consists of relatively small venues. This means they won't get paid much for their performances. Without the money to hire a crew, they often perform a variety of jobs besides the one they love.

The Scoop

Not all musicians have the means to tour. The Black Eyed Peas are now one of the most popular live acts on the planet, but this wasn't always the case. They originally formed in 1998, but didn't go on their first US tour until 2004.

FESTIVAL FEVER

Music festivals play an important role in the careers of live performers. For some, a great performance at a popular festival can put them on the music industry map. For others, a bad performance can mean the end of their career.

Festivals give musicians a rare chance to show off their performance skills to a wider audience and promote their own concert tours.

Thousands in a Field

Most festivals tend to take place over a long weekend, often in large parks or in the countryside. They often feature a number of stages, giving music fans a choice of bands at any one time. With up to ten slots on each stage every day, festivals may showcase as many as 200 bands over the span of three or four days.

Big Chance

Performers can attract new fans at music festivals. Unlike their own concerts, which are usually attended by established fans, they may be completely unknown to festival audiences. The stakes are very high. If they perform poorly, they risk the chance of receiving bad reviews. If they perform well, they could sell more CDs and gain a stronger following.

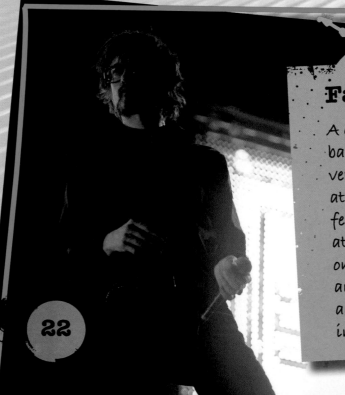

Famous Performance

A great festival performance can change a band's career. British indie band Pulp wasn't very well known when they were booked to play at the Glastonbury Festival in 1995. When festival headliners The Stone Roses canceled at the last minute, Pulp ended up filling in on the main stage. They delivered an energetic and faultless performance, winning over the audience. Soon after, they became major figures in the Britpop movement of the 1990s.

Iconic Appearances

Many stars have become famous for certain festival performances. Beyoncé was already well known when she **headlined** at Glastonbury in 2011, but her dazzling performance in front of 100,000 people boosted her reputation. Rock legend Jimi Hendrix will always be remembered for his performance at Woodstock in 1969. In 2006, The Flaming Lips interrupted their 2006 show at SXSW to allow two couples to get engaged on stage. And once, Rage Against the Machine took to the stage at Lollapalooza without any clothes on!

Missing in Action

Another festival appearance that sent shockwaves through the music world took place in 2008. Rapper M.I.A. shocked fans by retiring from playing live during her set at Bonnaroo in Tennessee. She canceled the rest of her world tour the very next day. She has since returned to the stage, and in 2012, performed with Madonna during the Super Bowl half-time show.

The Scoop

One of the most popular music events in the world, Lollapalooza introduced the idea of the traveling festival. In the 1990s and 2000s, Lollapalooza held events in US cities over the course of three months. Its lineup rarely changed from city to city. Now, Lollapalooza exists as a traditional festival. In 2014, it was held in Chile, Argentina, and Chicago.

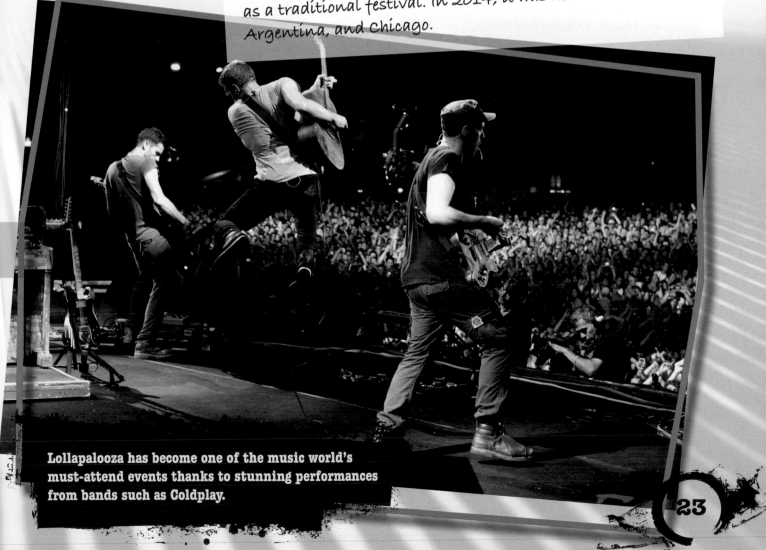

Lollapalooza has become one of the music world's must-attend events thanks to stunning performances from bands such as Coldplay.

Michael Eavis

Many business people have made a lot of money from music festivals. Perhaps the most famous example is British farmer Michael Eavis, who founded and still runs one of the biggest annual music events in the world: Glastonbury.

Humble Origins

Michael Eavis was born in 1935 into a family of dairy farmers. In the 1950s, he inherited his father's farm in Pilton, a small village near Glastonbury in Somerset, UK. For 15 years, he worked on the farm, selling his cows' milk to make a living.

Every few years, Michael Eavis takes a break. There was no Glastonbury Festival in 2012.

Inspiration

In 1969, Eavis visited the historic British city of Bath, where he stumbled across a free music festival. Called the Bath Festival of Blues, it featured performances by some of the most famous UK rock bands of the time. Excited by seeing thousands of people enjoying live music, he decided to host a festival at his farm.

TIMELINE: Michael Eavis

1935: Born in Dorset, UK

1958: Inherits Worthy Farm in Pilton, Somerset, from his father

1969: Attends the Bath Festival of Blues

1970: Hosts the first ever Glastonbury Festival at Worthy Farm

1986: The 10th Glastonbury Festival attracts a then record crowd of 60,000

2005: A record 153,000 tickets are sold for the year's festival

2010: Glastonbury Festival celebrates its 40th birthday

2011: Beyoncé becomes the first female R&B star to headline the event

Glastonbury One

The first ever Glastonbury Festival took place on Michael Eavis' farm in June 1970. Eavis booked all of the bands himself, helped build the stage, and organized the entire thing with the help of his wife, Jean. Entrance cost under two dollars and just over 1,500 people turned up.

Building a Reputation

Although early Glastonbury Festivals weren't a massive success, Eavis decided to stick with the idea. It paid off for him. By the early 1980s more than 60,000 people were heading to his farm every summer to hear some of the best bands in the world. As the years rolled on, the festival's reputation grew, and soon people were traveling from around the world to attend.

High Demand

Today, the Glastonbury Festival is one of the most popular live music events in the world. Demand for tickets is so high, the event usually sells out within hours of going on sale. It is now produced by Festival Republic, a music events company owned by Live Nation —the world's largest concert promotion organization.

After running the Glastonbury Festival almost single-handedly for 40 years, Michael Eavis is now assisted by his daughter, Emily.

Money-Maker

The Glastonbury Festival has made Michael Eavis a rich man. Although it is expensive to run, and takes up most of Eavis' and daughter Emily's time, it is worth it. For the 2014 festival 120,000 tickets sold out in 87 minutes.

Michael Eavis gives a large portion of his profits to charity. Many of the people who work at the event are volunteers, and their wages are also donated to charity. In 2008 alone, Eavis gave Oxfam (a charitable organization) over $319,000.

CHAPTER THREE

BEHIND THE SCENES

Although it's the performers who make their magic happen on stage, live music events would simply not exist without the dedication of people behind the scenes. From **road crew**, lighting specialists, and sound technicians to bus drivers and **tour managers**, everyone has a major role to play.

Many concerts would grind to a halt without the tireless work of the dedicated people behind the scenes, such as these sound technicians.

In Charge

The most important member of a performer's backroom team is the tour manager. This person has a lot of responsibility. As well as making sure the artist gets to the venue on time, the tour manager also has to deal with venue owners, book hotels, and sort out any problems that arise. This person must also supervise the entire backroom team.

Join the Crew

Most performers tour with a road crew. Members of the road crew are known as "roadies." These people do the bulk of the hard physical labor.

Sorting the Sound

Many rock and pop bands travel on tour with a number of sound technician specialists. These people have an understanding of how instruments and electrical equipment work. Rock bands may employ a guitar technician to look after their guitars, repair them if they break, and make sure they sound as good as they can.

Mix Master

One of the most important people at a concert is the sound technician who mans the **mixing desk**. Every instrument and microphone is plugged into the mixing desk. It's the sound technician's job to alter the volume of each instrument and adjust the microphone to get the best possible sound. This job responsibility lasts the duration of the concert.

Publicity and Security

On big tours, a **public relations** manager may travel with the band. It's their responsibility to handle all requests from journalists, radio stations, and television companies for interviews with the band. Celebrity artists may also have their own security guards. It's their job to keep the artist safe and make sure fans don't get too close.

Lights and Special Effects

Some musicians like to put on a light show at their concerts. To do this, they hire a lighting technician. It's their job to test out the lights and special effects beforehand. During the show, the lighting technician is in charge of switching the right lights on and off at the right time.

It can take many hours for lighting technicians to set up all of the special effects used in big concerts.

The Scoop

Big concert tours require a lot of people behind the scenes. The program for Lady Gaga's Monster Ball world tour listed more than 50 traveling staff members. Add in the number of uncredited roadies, **riggers**, set builders, and security staff, and the number of people involved in making each concert happen is likely to be near 100!

ROADIES

The life of a roadie isn't a glamorous one, but without their hard work and dedication, many concerts would never happen.

You and Your Crew

The word "roadie" comes from the term "road crew," the name given to the people behind the scenes who do all the physical work at concerts. There is no set position description for every roadie to follow, and the term is often loosely used to describe anyone who works on a tour and isn't a band member.

Many Duties

First and foremost, roadies are responsible for all of the equipment a band needs to perform. That means they load and unload instruments, **amplifiers**, and other heavy equipment from vans and trucks, take it to the stage, and set it up. When the performance is done, they go through the same process in reverse, making sure all the equipment is packed up and loaded back into the vans and trucks.

Different Roles

Not all roadies haul equipment, set up lights, and build the stage. They may be in charge of selling merchandise such as T-shirts and CDs to fans, or cooking food for the band and other tour staff to eat. Others may act as personal assistants to the tour manager or band members. Depending on the size and scale of the tour, the tasks a roadie might have to perform are wide and varied.

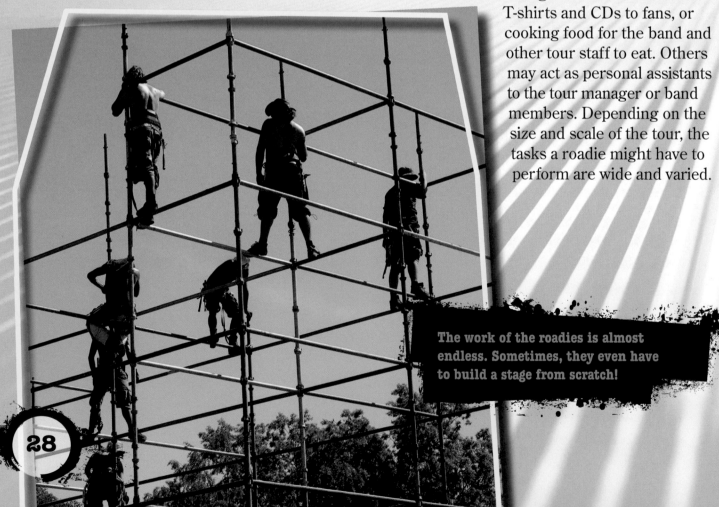

The work of the roadies is almost endless. Sometimes, they even have to build a stage from scratch!

Mobile Living

In between gigs, roadies travel together with other tour staff on a sleeper coach bus. This is a bus with bunk beds, a bathroom, a kitchen, and a place to relax. Usually up to 20 roadies will share one bus.

Tough Break

Being a roadie is a hard job, but sometimes it can offer a faster route into the music business. The pay isn't great, but you get to work with a band and watch them perform. If you're an ambitious musician, you can learn a lot from working as a roadie, at least what it takes to make a concert tour impressive and smoothly run.

The Scoop

It's not uncommon for roadies to fill in on stage when a band member is ill. Stuart Morgan, bass technician for U2's Adam Clayton, filled in for his boss at a concert in Sydney in 1993, while Metallica roadie John Marshall has joined the band on stage numerous times as a stand-in for James Hetfield. In 2005, Metallica's management demanded that Hetfield stop skateboarding on tour as he'd injured himself too many times!

Roadie to Rock Star

A number of rock stars worked as roadies before going on to worldwide musical success. Oasis guitarist Noel Gallagher worked as a roadie for early-1990s British band Inspiral Carpets, while Nirvana roadie Ben Shepherd ended up joining grunge band Soundgarden.

Soundgarden's Ben Shepherd is just one of a string of famous musicians who started their music careers as roadies.

GIG BUSINESS

It's not just performers who can make serious amounts of money from live music. Booking agents and concert promoters can also get very rich from concert tours.

In the Book

Booking agents are the first connection a venue owner would make to hire a musician. Booking agents sign up bands they would like to represent, promising them gigs all over the country or even the world. When a performer tells their booking agent they would like to tour, it is up to the agent to get them gigs.

Paid to Get the Gig

Booking agents are not always popular with venue owners and concert promoters. It's the booking agent's job to ensure the bands they represent get good gigs that pay well. To make this happen, booking agents are usually paid on a **commission** basis. This means a percentage of the fee paid to hire a band—usually between 10 and 20 percent—goes directly to the agent.

Get an Agent

There are very few booking agents who work solely with one band, or even on their own.

Booking agents spend a lot of time on the telephone, fielding calls from promoters wanting to book the bands they represent.

The live music scene is dominated by a handful of big booking agencies. These companies employ a number of agents, each of whom represents a group of artists.

Big Players

In recent years, the concert and tour promotion industry has been dominated by a small number of enormous companies. The biggest of these is US corporation Live Nation. Their competitors include the worldwide group AEG Live and UK-based companies SJM Concerts, Metropolis Music, and Mean Fiddler.

Live Music for a Living

Booking agents do not organize concerts. This is the job of concert promoters. They call agents to find bands to play at their events. Most concert promoters start out organizing gigs in their local area, working with agents, and hiring suitable venues. They pay the band's fee and sometimes the cost to rent the venue up front, gambling that they will make enough money from ticket sales to cover their costs.

Tour Gamble

The next step for many concert promoters is tour promotion. This means organizing an entire tour for a band. Usually, a tour promoter agrees to pay a performer's booking agent a set fee to play a number of concerts. It's then up to the promoter to book the venues, promote the concerts, and sell tickets.

Ticket sales are the most important thing to concert promoters— without them, they won't be able to make a living.

The Scoop

Concert promoters AEG lost out on millions of dollars when pop legend Michael Jackson died. The company had booked the singer to play more than 30 shows at the massive O2 Arena in London, but he passed away before the shows could take place. They were forced to refund thousands of ticket holders.

KING OF POP
MICHAEL JACKSON
THIS IS IT

Live Nation

Live Nation is the single biggest live music events corporation in the world. Since its beginning in 2005, it has grown rapidly to become one of the music industry's most dominant companies.

Clear Idea

Live Nation grew out of a US company called Clear Channel Communications. Since the 1970s, Clear Channel had built up a vast empire of radio stations, outdoor advertising (poster sites on bus shelters and enormous roadside billboards), and concert venues. In 2005, Clear Channel's board of directors decided to transfer their concert promotion business to a new company, which they called Live Nation.

Artists on Board

Owning a vast network of venues was just the beginning. In 2007, Live Nation secured tour contracts for some of the world's biggest artists. Jay-Z, Madonna, U2, and Shakira all signed on to a new management company called Live Nation Artists. They promised to play concerts exclusively for Live Nation in return for multimillion-dollar fees.

Signing top performers such as Rihanna has helped Live Nation become one of the richest entertainment companies in the world.

RIHANNA
LOUD TOUR
JUNE 6 & 7

TICKETMASTER.CA | 1.855.985.5000

LG

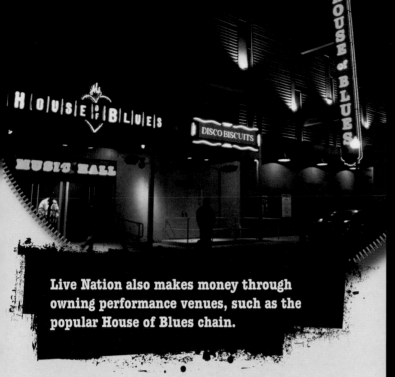

Live Nation also makes money through owning performance venues, such as the popular House of Blues chain.

Live Nation also owns a number of other companies that operate concert spaces or run music festivals. These include SFX Entertainment, which owns 135 venues around the world, and Festival Republic, the company that produces UK festivals such as Download and Latitude.

Shrewd Business

The deals done with these global stars are worth far more than their recording contracts, traditionally the best money-makers. Live Nation now effectively manages these artists, looking after all interests apart from recording contracts. They plan to launch a record label to rival the five big "majors" of the industry.

Ticket Deal

Live Nation now dominates the worldwide event ticket sales market. In 2009, it merged with the world's biggest ticketing company, Ticketmaster, to form Live Nation Entertainment. With everything under one roof, a sizeable amount of money can be earned.

Major Player

Live Nation Entertainment also dominates the live music market, both in the US and worldwide. Every year, it promotes or produces some 22,000 concerts, selling more than $50 million worth of tickets. Because of this and other interests, the company is now worth billions of dollars.

Unpopular

Not all music fans are happy with Live Nation. They say the company charges too much for tickets, and it has a stranglehold on the live music scene. In 2012, many Madonna fans complained because her concert tickets cost upward of $150.

TIMELINE: Live Nation

1972: Clear Channel Communications forms in Los Angeles, California
2005: Live Nation forms from Clear Channel's concert promotion business
2006: Live Nation buys the House of Blues chain of concert venues
2007: Live Nation Artists forms and signs Madonna

2008: U2, Jay-Z, and Shakira all sign to Live Nation Artists in $100 million deals
2009: Live Nation merges with Ticketmaster to form Live Nation Entertainment
2012: Live Nation Entertainment announces major world tours from Madonna, LMFAO, and Lady Gaga

CHAPTER FOUR

ULTIMATE CONCERTS

When a performer becomes a household name, demand for tickets for their concerts around the world can be enormous. An ordinary tour of medium-sized venues isn't enough. To satisfy demand, artists play huge arenas, **amphitheatres**, and stadiums.

Long Haul

When an artist reaches this level of fame, nothing less than a full world tour will do. For major bands this means performing concerts worldwide over a long period of time, sometimes up to three years.

Many Legs

To make life easier for the performer and road crew, long world tours are usually divided into "legs." Each leg focuses on a different continent or group of countries, and the entire crew gets a small break at the end of each one.

How Long?

Just how long a tour takes depends on the number of dates in each leg, and the size of the country or continent the concerts are being played in. Frequently, artists on long tours may play a two-month block of dates in the US, have a couple of weeks off, and then spend a month elsewhere. By the end of a two-year world tour, a performer may have played more than 100 different concerts.

Playing enormous venues allows top bands to accompany their performances with expensive pyrotechnics displays, such as this one from an AC/DC concert.

Private Parties

Many of the world's top stars have a lucrative sideline performing at private parties thrown by super-rich individuals. Beyoncé (right), Usher, Mariah Carey, and Elton John have all been paid more than $1 million by billionaires to perform short sets at weddings, social events, and exclusive parties.

Beyoncé has performed at a variety of different venues—some low-key with 50 guests, others at sold-out arenas.

Toil and Trouble

Organizing a big world tour is very hard work. Even with time off between legs, it is a tough task. On these big tours, many performers bring their own sets for the stages, which need to be built before the concert. Afterward, they need to be taken down and packed away before they can be transported to the next gig.

Rich Rewards

World tours of stadiums and huge arenas cost a great deal of money to put on. Transporting many thousands of tons of equipment and a large road crew around the world is not cheap. However, with up to 50,000 tickets being sold for each concert, it is still possible for an artist to finish their tour millions of dollars richer.

The Scoop

Pop legend Michael Jackson's *History* world tour between 1996 and 1997 is one of the most successful of all time. Jackson played 82 dates in 18 months, selling more than 4.5 million tickets! In 2012, Lady Gaga announced the *Born This Way Ball* world tour, featuring more than 100 performances over an 18-month period. This may be one of the most successful tours of all time, raking in over $350 million in ticket sales.

U2 360° World Tour

The world's most successful tour to date is the *360°* tour by Irish rockers U2. Many of their previous tours, including *Zoo TV* (1992–93) and *Vertigo* (2005–06), broke attendance records. Over 3.5 million people went to concerts on the *Vertigo* tour, making it one of the ten highest grossing tours of all time. But for their next tour, *360°*, U2 wanted to go even bigger.

New Concept

U2 wanted the shows on their *360°* tour to be spectacular. And they delivered. They asked their set designer to come up with a new concept for the stage they would perform on. He decided to make the stage round, with an enormous sound system and towering video screen positioned above it on a giant, four-legged metal claw.

Rock First

The claw-like set was the largest tour stage set ever built, stretching over 165 feet (51 m) high. It was incredibly complicated to set up and take apart, so three different versions were used on the tour. Each of the claw sets cost over $15 to 20 million. Between gigs, it took a fleet of 120 trucks to transport all the parts by road.

U2's record-breaking *360°* tour saw the band playing to crowds of 60,000 a night.

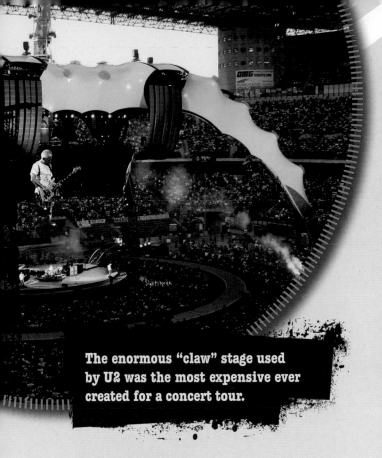

The enormous "claw" stage used by U2 was the most expensive ever created for a concert tour.

this high number of workers and the difficulty in assembling the stage, each concert cost about $750,000 to put on.

Seven Legs

U2 began the *360°* tour in Barcelona, Spain, on June 30, 2009. By the time the tour ended in July 2011 in Moncton, Canada, the band had played 110 concerts all over the world. This included separate legs dedicated to South America, Australasia, Africa, and two trips to both Europe and North America.

Live Online

During the tour, U2 became the first band to broadcast one of their concerts live over the video-sharing website YouTube. Over 10 million people from 128 countries tuned in to watch the Rose Bowl show in Pasadena, California, on October 25, 2009.

Video Stars

It wasn't just the stage itself that was complicated. The giant video screen that formed part of the claw stage set was made up of thousands of individual sections, all connected by 3,000 electrical cables.

Records Tumble

Due to the enormous costs of staging the concerts, it wasn't until the later legs of the tour that U2 began to make money. In total, U2's *360°* tour made more than $736 million in ticket sales, making it the most successful rock tour of all time. An astonishing 7.4 million people attended the 110 concerts—another Guinness World Record.

Huge Crew

The number of people required to make the tour run smoothly was enormous. There were more than 130 people in U2's traveling road crew. The band's tour promoters, Live Nation, also recruited up to 120 people to work part-time at each venue. Because of

TIMELINE: U2

1976: Four school friends form U2 in Dublin, Ireland
1982: U2 set out on *War*, their first world tour
2005: Record-breaking 131-date *Vertigo* world tour begins

2009: *360°* tour begins in Barcelona, Spain
2010: *360°* tour visits Australia, New Zealand, and Europe
2011: *360°* tour finishes in Moncton, Canada

SHOW SPECTACULAR

Some of the most spectacular concerts of all time are not part of tours by individual artists, but rather big charity events featuring many different bands and artists. The most famous examples of these are Live Aid and Live 8.

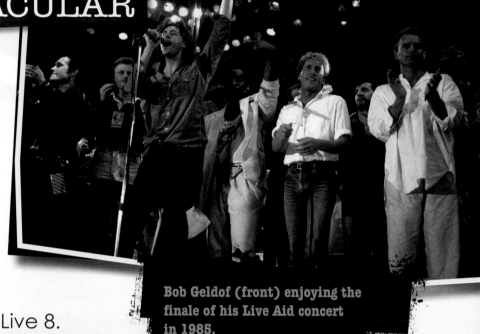

Bob Geldof (front) enjoying the finale of his Live Aid concert in 1985.

Just Cause

In 1984 and 1985, hundreds of thousands of people in Africa were dying of starvation. Pop stars Bob Geldof and Midge Ure wanted to do something about it, so they decided to raise money to help. They put on two massive concerts on the same day in July 1985—one at Wembley Stadium in London, UK, the other at JFK Stadium in Philadelphia, Pennsylvania.

Begging Calls

To make the Live Aid concerts a success, Geldof and Ure needed to make sure all of the world's biggest pop and rock stars were involved. They spent months calling stars and begging them to take part. Almost all said yes.

Enormous Success

Live Aid in 1985 was one of the biggest pop and rock events of all time. Millions of people around the world tuned in via television to watch live performances from artists such as Madonna, Paul McCartney, Run-D.M.C., Stevie Wonder, The Rolling Stones, Bob Dylan, Queen, and Lionel Richie.

The Scoop

At the Live Aid concert in Philadelphia, Rolling Stones' members Ronnie Wood and Keith Richards appeared on stage with Bob Dylan. When one of Dylan's guitar strings broke, Ronnie Wood passed him his guitar. For the rest of the performance, Wood had to make do with playing air guitar!

Millions Raised

In the US and the UK, television viewers were urged to pick up the phone and pledge whatever they could afford. Millions of people did, and the next day Bob Geldof announced that over $72 million had been raised for charity.

Playing Again

In 2005, 20 years after the original Live Aid concerts, Bob Geldof decided to do it all over again. This time, the concerts would be used to persuade governments to write-off billions of dollars worth of debts owed by poor African countries. It worked; the world's wealthiest countries reached a landmark agreement at the Gleneagles summit in July 2005.

Big Stars

Just like Live Aid in 1985, Live 8 featured performances by many top stars. Snoop Dogg, Green Day, The Thrills, The Killers, Scissor Sisters, Shakira, Coldplay, and Kanye West all appeared, playing sets at concerts in London, Philadelphia, Moscow, Berlin, Paris, Edinburgh, and Tokyo.

Record Makers

A small number of performers appeared at both Live Aid in 1985 and Live 8 in 2005. These included U2, Madonna, Elton John, Sting, The Who, Paul McCartney, and Bob Geldof.

Ethiopian Birhan Woldu appeared as a starving child in a video broadcast at the 1985 Live Aid concerts. She joined Madonna on stage at Live 8 20 years later.

BEYOND THE BAND

There has always been more to live performance than just singing and playing music well. The world's best live performers are not just great musicians, but also fantastic entertainers.

From Good to Great

An amazing show is what separates good performers from great ones. If a band can play their instruments well, they will give a good performance. Bands that put in great performances do so with flair and style, adding extra elements to make their concerts more memorable.

This giant moving robot figure offered a spectacular stage setting for Take That's 2011 *Progress* tour.

The Scoop

Sometimes, getting the audience very excited can go very wrong. At the Woodstock festival in 1999, some members of the crowd started to break stuff when Limp Bizkit played their song, "Break Stuff."

Spectacular Events

In the last 30 years, many performers have turned their concerts into spectacular audio-visual experiences by using elements more often found at the theater. These include costume changes, different sets for different segments of the show, dancers, firework displays, and dazzling special effects. For example, Take That's 2011 *Progress* live tour featured huge robot figures that lowered band members onto the stage, as well as towering video screens, dancers, and award-winning light displays.

Trend Setter

Since Madonna's pioneering tours in the 1980s, many other artists have taken a similar approach to their concerts and pulled out all the stops. Most pop artists—particularly solo performers—now surround themselves with dancers and wear many different outfits during performances.

Gaga Super Shows

In recent years, numerous acts have excelled at this type of musical extravaganza. The most famous is Lady Gaga, who developed a passion for **audio-visual** shows during her time working as a dancer in New York clubs. Now, her shows feature multiple costume changes, sets designed by leading artists, and a troupe of more than 20 dancers. Another artist who likes to put on a spectacular show is Beyoncé.

Solo pop performers, such as Lady Gaga, often liven up their shows by using stunning dance routines.

Costume Changes

One of the first artists to put on an elaborate show was Madonna. She set a trend on her *Who's That Girl* tour in 1987 by having many different costume changes. These costumes were made by some of the world's most famous fashion designers. During performances, Madonna also took part in exciting dance routines. She called the show "a musical theater extravaganza."

Beyoncé flies through the air on a **high-wire** at one of her sensational concerts.

BIGGER, STRONGER, LONGER

The live music scene is in good shape right now. For the first time since recorded music became popular in the 1950s, pop and rock performers are earning more money from selling concert tickets than CDs or music downloads. Live music is back.

Changing Times

Traditionally, almost all bands and singers made their name on the live music circuit. By building up a following through a steady stream of concerts, they might be lucky enough to earn a recording contract.

Then, every time they made a new album, they would go on tour to promote it. Playing live helped them to sell records or CDs, which is where they made the most money.

Live Music Revival

Now, the process has changed. Many artists still build up their reputation through live performances and then put out CDs and downloads, but now those music releases are little more than ads for their concerts. Around the world, sales of music releases have dropped significantly because of illegal downloads, yet concert ticket sales have been rising across the board. More people attend live music events than ever before.

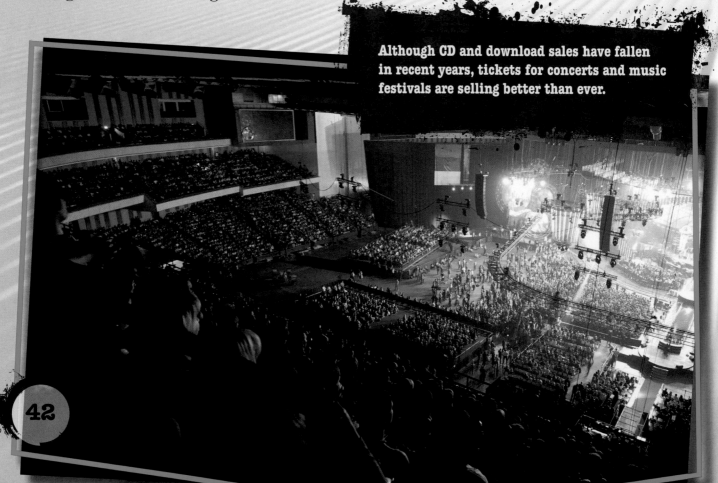

Although CD and download sales have fallen in recent years, tickets for concerts and music festivals are selling better than ever.

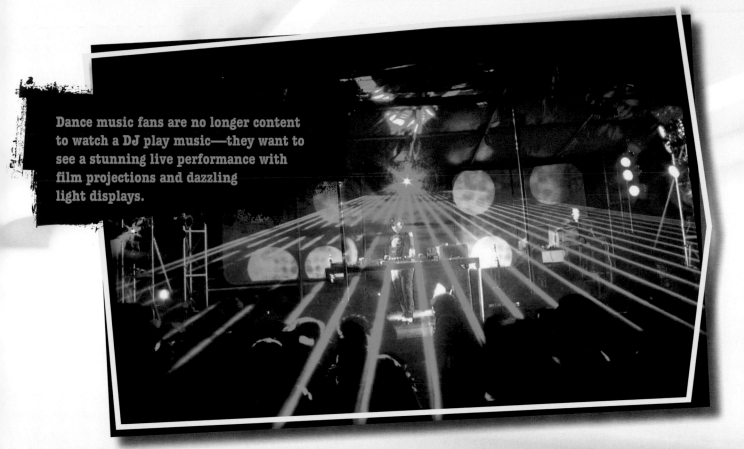

Dance music fans are no longer content to watch a DJ play music—they want to see a stunning live performance with film projections and dazzling light displays.

Big Deals

It's no wonder that some musicians have decided to be managed by tour promotion companies such as the massive Live Nation group. U2, Madonna, Jay-Z, Lady Gaga, and Shakira do not need to be tied down to a record label. They can devote more of their time touring the world, earning millions in the process. New CDs will only be released when they have a tour planned. In the future, more performers may sign similar deals.

The Scoop

Some performers decide not to tour and instead perform a run of shows at one big venue. Legendary singer Prince started a trend when he signed to play 21 concerts in August and September 2007 at the 20,000-capacity O2 Arena in London. Every concert sold out.

On the Rise

The popularity of live events can be seen at a local level. Despite warnings from musicians that smaller venues have been closing down in recent years, figures suggest that there are now more concerts every year than ever before. Local live music scenes are getting stronger, which is good news for ambitious young bands and singers.

Dance Live

Even dance and electronic artists have jumped on the live performance bandwagon. Before, dance musicians would have been content to make records and perform DJ sets. Now, more and more are developing live shows. Thanks to changes in computer technology, they can re-create their tracks live on stage.

GLOSSARY

acoustic music made with instruments that do not require electronic equipment

amateurs people who do something as a hobby

amphitheatres open-air concert venues, usually with seating arranged in a semi-circle facing the stage

amplifiers enormous speakers that allow the audience to hear what the band is playing

apprenticeship the process of learning a skill or trade, for example, how to become a good guitarist or singer

audio-visual the combination of sound and moving images or light displays

backing band the musicians who provide the musical backing for an artist

band manager someone who looks after the business affairs of a musical group

busking playing music in public, for example, on the street or at a train station, to earn money

chords groups of musical notes played at the same time on a guitar or keyboard

commission being paid a wage that varies depending on how successful you are

concert promoter someone who makes a living from organizing concerts

digital sampler a machine that allows you to copy small pieces of recorded music and alter them to make something new

electronic musicians people who make music with computers instead of conventional instruments

fan base people who are dedicated followers of a certain band, singer, rapper, or style of music

gig musicians' slang for concert

headline to play the most high profile performance slot at a festival or event

high-wire a taut wire stretched high above an audience that an act performs on

hip-hop a type of street music that originated from the US in the 1980s

house band a small group of musicians employed to play music in theatres or television studios

influential someone who changes the way people think or do something

instrumentals pieces of music that feature no vocals

integral of vital importance

mixing desk a piece of equipment used for monitoring sound levels at a concert or in a recording studio

musicals a type of play featuring singing and dancing, usually performed in theatres

press officer the person who deals with requests from journalists for interviews with musicians

promoters people who plan and publicize concerts or club nights

public relations the process of managing a person, group, or business's public image and profile

R&B rhythm and blues

recording contract a legal agreement between a musician and a company in which the company agrees to pay the musician to record songs and albums

residency when a band or artist performs regularly at a venue, usually weekly or monthly

riffs rock musicians' slang for short sequences of chords or musical melodies

riggers "roadies" who specialize in setting up lights and stage sets

road crew also known as "roadies," this is the collective name for all the people, except the artist, who work on a concert tour

session musicians musicians for hire who are not attached to one particular band

soundcheck the process of testing out instruments and microphones before a performance to make sure everything is working correctly

synthesizer an electronic keyboard that allows users to change the way it sounds using various control buttons and dials

tour a series of concerts in different places

tour manager the person who makes sure a concert tour runs smoothly

venues places where entertainment is performed

VIP guests VIP stands for "very important people"—usually sponsors, friends, and record label executives

FURTHER READING

Books

Bob Tulipan. *Rockin' in the New World: Taking Your Band from the Basement to the Big Time* (Sterling, 2011).

Jen Jones. *Becoming a Pop Star* (Capstone Press, 2008).

Matt Anniss. *Start a Band* (Arcturus Publishing, 2012).

Paul Rutter. *The Music Industry Handbook* (Routledge, 2011).

Websites

Get advice about how to get your band or solo performances showcased at:
www.bbc.co.uk/music/introducing/advice

Read top tips about perfecting your act at:
www.cheapadviceonmusic.com/category/live-sound/

Great information and advice for musicians can be found at:
www.independentmusicadvice.com

INDEX